AF489694

Second Chance Somedays

Joe Albanese

Copyright© 2023 Joe Albanese
ISBN: 978-93-95224-83-3

First Edition: 2023
Rs. 200/-

Cyberwit.net
HIG 45 Kaushambi Kunj, Kalindipuram
Allahabad - 211011 (U.P.) India
http://www.cyberwit.net
Tel: +(91) 9415091004
E-mail: info@cyberwit.net

No part of this book may be reproduced or transmitted in any form or by any means, electronic, mechanical, photocopying, or otherwise, without the express written consent of Joe Albanese.

Printed at VCORE.

Contents

Trading Post at the Edge of Known

Empty more mistaken pearl
to curl fate

and find oneself

somewhere with
no stars
and no fear,
no knots and
no ends

The varied cost not haggled,
just peaked and tipped

Traverse naught and koan, and
trust the seed into the flame

leaving only an epitaph of sand

Go without stars
Go without fear

Lapsed in the Grain

Its light grows on summer being—hoped
and demented, forced and forgotten

Its hunger hides in lamenting autumn—placed
and re-placed, gone from the donning

Heroes rise on fallen thunder—cupped
ears dropping, lifetimes laughing

Guarded by the morning humming—lost
in damnation but found in its wishing

The year of our lord was a far-off not coming—torn
from the ashes, learned from its nothings

Hope was born from the hazing unfounded—burnt
in asylum, caught in denial

Vengeful still lies in the kindness ungrowing—lapsed
in the grain of what once was unwanted

Made Up in Laughing

Frame half-open windows
Slip out of billows
Stomp on the sunlight
    stamped in the sidewalk
Dry and kind

Call off a shadow
Tripped up in meadow
The sere breath is casting,
    made up in laughing
Holding all chance others left behind

When day drops to fair-low
Return not its sparrow
Its echo's in moonlight,
    verve in the clockwork
Draped in the caul of what we can't unwind

Truth in Being

I've garnished my
plausibilities until they've been
sifted and sifted again. Trapped
in mock missionary, lost
under the brazen cloud of
yesteryear.
I've been tight-roped…then
I walked it off. Keep
me in the now, relaxed in
the warmth of
wandering could-bes—free
from the debt of false
hopes; remade in the verve
of questioning—replaced
by the truth in being.

Warning: Rant Commencing

Not in the wishing well do I sing,
but in the jagged edges of a dying
star. (The reciprocal use of what
I've amassed has gone unnoticed.)
It is in that humble giant that I
daydream, turned inside out for
all to see. Bare and blind I call out
to strangers for guidance, yet all
I find are empty handshakes and
forgotten promises. Forgive me
while I weep; it is not in you I
seek assistance but in the calling
itself—the never-answer be
answer enough.

The Pronation of Shangri La

Bellowed to the threat of any falling leaves
Softcore Shangri La is gone but far from freed
Caught in the tired idea that petrichor is wrong

Upended by some heathen in the scattered steam
A valley that's been dried out yet not quite cleared
Cross-eyed, unremarkable garden forms a path

Retreaded by many so-and-sos just like me
To the beacon of kingdom con and its seams
Whatever's being kicked up stains twice, and

there's no going back

A Second Day

Midnight crown and daunted growing.
I'd rather face the night and earn a
second day. Waves and waves of
could-be hopes and next-time semblances
of a tomorrow coming. A wrong turn sent
me here, in the dark, away from ease and
establishment. Away from comfort and
beauty to this darkness, *this* darkness—
only kept by sight unfounded. I see those
monsters up ahead. But only by light
do we see. There must be some more,
past the gruesome hold this dark has
over me. So I press on: I'd rather face
the night and earn a second day.

Call Me an Aside

Call it an aside in
me, there
are some delights I find in
my way, to warm an
un-constellation—my
time in humiliated conversion

It's not divine or
wanted, but
reestablished every night
and day
in retro finesse and
vertigo

Turn me around, turn me
around to wanton
daydream
and hold
me there, where I
can call me home,
where I can call
something mine

Sway and Sway

Sway and sway the birds away

the vine, it grows like autumn slumber,
heroes died along the way

weakness is my fallen glowing,
just like villains kept at bay

trick-or-treat the youthful sending,
Pleiades owes the warmth come May

velvet houses are my queue unknowing,
sway and sway the birds away

Just Another Midnight

Summer breaks to fall, and
I know that things
can change—I see it

But this is just another
midnight

A turning of the tide, they
say, is
coming, and for a brief

moment of hope I

think one day I'll be laughing and
say to myself, "I'm laughing. Thank
God I'm laughing."

But this is just another midnight

Above the Fire

Above the fire is
where every phrase gets
coined. Just like the spider
walks that
carful line, we are just a
momentary lapse
from miracle or disaster.
Call me a coward
and I'll call you a fool.
This is where I make my
home; this is where life
is won or lost.

What I Think What Is

Locked in a sermon that shreds me apart
Inspired by Genesis; created from loss

Both drained and diluted—my stories don't start
They just reappear and then tilt till they cross

It is forged but unstable, a blessing I draw
A fable of memory and a future that's wrong

What I wish were a lesson is merely a flaw
The truth is not welcomed, the daydreams belong

Second Chance Somedays

White lights and
phantom glows—how did
I dine in the dark? When did
I escape that cerement?

Did something push me in
this right direction—from
when I only held
peripherals—maybe I fell
here myself.

Time-lapse from night
to day. Scattered in the
wind there,
lost and found, reestablished
in the hope of
second chance somedays.

Another Dream, Another Chance

An angel fare, my modern scream—a day
within a day
I lost myself and found you there—within
the wild fray

Hope! The return of desperate prayer—luck,
anointment, haze
Another dream, another chance—one more
along the way

Cairn at 34

I'm not old, I don't think

My face is young still but grey hair
is no longer scattered

I'm 15 and 50 at the same time

I piss too often
or can't remember if I just did
—either way a sign

Age and I inch closer
as friends taper off and
the effort to remember names ends
in vain

I'll be 34 next week, and this is just my
system to mark my way.

Port of Call

Damp stains
Beneath a starlit sky

The gutter is calling
For all memory; it's time

Let go
The winds already fled to leave behind

A world not falling
Port of call and not again

Just Off Communication

I speak
with forced cadence or
apathetic empathy into my
phone.
Outside, I listen to the
never-quite connected

There's no ring or vibration

Not yet

Not until the other
pieces together what could be
an ironic
disposition or genuine
aptitude

Return to sender:

Our always-waiting gets
the blood rushing
until it peaks, then
cools like lava. Black,
lifeless emotion,
ready to go back
to the task

Thank God we
don't know each other

Not really.

Slant-Rhyme With Me

Won't you stay and slant-
      rhyme with me?
Sometimes—lost in omni-pain—I
bleed right
      up the wall, then
get doused in stain.
      Call it what you will, it's all
the same—at times I need
what's in the mud, and all you
      seized.
What's left in me?
Maybe I just need a moment
tomorrow to breathe, but not
      today—
      today is for slant rhyme.
Won't you stay and
      slant-rhyme with me?

Quit Complaining

My expression folded, my hands
are dry, someone left me along
the way. But everyone has done
some begging until they too are
made of ground. My future is
unfolding, my treble sees undoing,
what happened to my promised
crown? This is today, this is
tomorrow, this is what I've waited
for.

These New Shoes

I walked once of twice in
these new shoes
then back to old
In form
There's comfort there, I suppose
Worn in yet wearing thin
Push it more
until strain or break
But back to old
There's comfort there

Expat

Bound to North
Not home nor far
Made by escape,
A hope to fight

Trust lantern lost
Believed or touched
Fade made by dark,
And light by light

When cold turns warmth
And prayer divides
Be either sail in storm,
Or spark from night

Well, Fuck

Well fuck is a profane word
I sometimes use
Ok, maybe more
It's a simple song
The most economical
of words
Too concise and broad
to lose itself in muck
Bookends or bookended, it
stands strong
Because you had to see,
had to read
And you've been there to
exclaim, expel, and
invariably explain

On the Beach

Dress my mouth
in orange sin
Bless my tongue,
believe in luck
Give your hand,
we'll walk on glass
Tell your notes
across those sands
Place a love
beneath the sun
Capture warmth
and breathe you in
Water wait,
taste my ledge
It's overcome
and not replaced

If Not For Today

Wait—did you hear that—that
subtle silence, careening
over the edge?
Lap up that happenstance
and drown those
misconceptions.
Trap misdirection and reverse
the impossibility. Force
and forge, then
gallantly accept. What
is tomorrow
if not for today?

Its Winds Still Blow From Time to Time

It comes like that,
with sheer weight that invariably
dismisses
all other thought. So
I grapple and claw to hold
ground in my mind
that has
been compromised each time
prior.
There is no taming this tempest
in my head; it can only
be set loose from time to time,
and I must remind myself
when ropes
and shackles
meet their brink. And so
I let those waves
crash there, taking me in
its throes—knowing
and not knowing the storm
has passed
so long ago. I myself
am merely on shores—watching,
waiting for
the end of the storm's
exhale.

From Temptress to Tempest

There he lies, there he dies;
there he spends his days. Cut
away from "what's your sign?"
to where he is broken in.
Something's under his skin,
what some would call a dive.
There he lies, there he dies;
there he spends his days. He
plays life with quarters—a
quarter of what it is: a rain
of muted speech. From
temptress to tempest:
there he lies, there he dies;
there he spends his days.

With Ease

I could fade away with ease.
Too many people say
I'm crazed—I swear I'm
psycho-neutral. My eyes outside
my head—I blink—I'm effervescent.
The lies make me search
for the data stream, I
I find it's not quite consequential.

And I fade away with ease.

Take some notes and
burn the scented. There are times
my mind seems codependent.
Lost in the crime of
a blended seam, I call, where
is my old mentor? Gone, like me.
So I fade away
with ease. With ease.

City Lights

Mind the wall not coming down
But something wrong
A gentle breeze
    Found all my seams
Climb; I climb beyond a crowd
To gain ground—the day's already over
I see city lights
    They don't betray me

Home, it's not far gone
Left and cold, a radio believes
The hunger belongs
    It all can't be a dream
Yesterday's rain still fogs the scene
An edifice an empty song relays
Those scattered city lights
    They don't betray me

A sun doesn't come this way
Can I love me not fall apart?
I can't be bereaved
    Unmanned belfry doesn't scream
Behind the toppled mountain I draw
Hear not a single call
But those city lights
    They don't betray me

Cut Shaving

The shards of blanket comfort
are all that remain—what framing work
this is, what demeaning work this has
become—begging like the hen baking bread.
A subaltern on the verge of demotion. Our
what and only-ifs have stenciled a paint by
numbers. What if I lack the proper color?
Neither of us has seen the distance, and now
we seep through ourselves. That and stained
vermillion are all that remain on the tile floor.

Ghost at Dawn

Fade into night with rising ghost,
shed wait for run and tumble to
a whimper kept at bay
and break to,
and break to
An autumn found my own and fine
here and here and now and now
and fine
the dawn breaks to,
the dawn breaks to
Ghost in pane above/below
may I follow through, or try
together with no hands held
I will follow and ghost as
the dawn breaks to,
as we break to dawn

You Know Me Too Well

My emblem
is a jagged smiley face
transcribed at the bottom
of a suicide note.
There it sits and renders,
there it mocks with taunting
silver linings.
It's a signature, a calling card.
It is Orion the hunter, it
is lies and truth. It is hope.
It is me.

Light on This Side of Mind

Light on this side of mind
In standard ground
Re-play the scene
MOS (or without sound)

There's more to come
No more to right
Design a loft, not a dry note
Never the risen knight

Just chosen of the mind
Your new motif
Settle home and light
Where darkness be no thief

Part of My Story Will Always Be Dark

Part of my story will always be dark;
those ever-nights
and non-stops, those always theres
and forever nots.
Part of that story will never end;
those smiles-be-gones and
cried dreams a lot.
Part of my story will always be dark;
but that is just part of my story…
while part of it's not.

Pieced Together

Born from the
after-light, examined by the
distant star.

Caressed and forgotten by
the once-winter nightfall.

Guard myself and tinker
with it until
jigsawed with a chainsaw.

I've been tampered with by
some unknown
god or wizard or
chance, spit up here
where gold
crackles piece me together.

I am holding. I am stronger
than before.

On the Dock of Infinity

Laced in petrichor, the hymn of
starlight catches me.
In the violet stem of long-dead
nebulae I
wait, dumbfounded by the
walk, tight-roped
and undone. Delighted
by the possibility, I follow the
far-off lantern—its calling
flickers.
Do I pick up the pace or slow
down? Draped in the fear
of a finale fading,
I press on. There, on the dock of
infinity, water whispers
to me, "We're all gonna get
there someday."

Acknowledgments

Some of these poems were first published in various literary magazines and journals. I thank them for their support.

Be About It Zine — "Call Me An Aside" and "Part of My Story Will Always Be Dark"

The Big Windows Review — "Pieced Together"

The Bosphorus Review — "Trading Post at the Edge of Known"

Ink Pantry — "Sway and Sway" and "Another Dream, Another Chance"

The Metaworker — "Cut Shaving"

Poetry Super Highway — "Well, Fuck"

The Ramingo's Porch — "A Second Day"

Scarlet Leaf Review — "On the Beach," "If Not For Today," and "Truth in Being"

Tipton Poetry Journal — "Above the Fire"

Whistling Shade — "On the Dock of Infinity"

www.ingramcontent.com/pod-product-compliance
Lightning Source LLC
Chambersburg PA
CBHW031005180726
47993CB00018B/1578